D1612400

GREAT EVENTS IN AUSTRALIA'S HISTORY

ALAN BOARDMAN & ROLAND HARVEY

THE FIRST FLEET · The Crossing of the Blue Mountains · Eureka Stockade

THE FIVE MILE PRESS
379 Smith Street
Fitzroy Victoria 3065 Australia

First Published 1985
Reprinted 1987
©The Five Mile Press 1985

Illustrated by Roland Harvey
Printed and bound in Hong Kong by
Dai Nippon Printing Company Ltd

National Library of Australia Cataloguing-in-Publication data

Boardman, Alan.
Great events in Australia's history.

ISBN 0 86788 072 4.

1. Australia — History — Juvenile literature.
I. Harvey, Roland, 1945-. II. Title.

994.02

THE FIRST FLEET

ALAN BOARDMAN   ROLAND HARVEY

London 1783 – for many a city of poverty and despair. Food and shelter were scarce and expensive, few people had jobs and many were forced to steal in order to feed themselves and their families. The narrow, dirty streets were crowded with beggars, pickpockets and all manner of desperate men, women and children.

John Hudson, a chimney sweep from Middlesex, was arrested whilst breaking into a house to commit a burglary. He was sent for trial at the Old Bailey.

The penalty for burglary was death but because of his age, Hudson's sentence was reduced to seven years transportation. John Hudson was nine years old.

With British gaols filled to overflowing the government had, for a number of years, been transporting its unwanted criminals to America but with the 1776 War of Independence, that practice came to an end.

As the crime rate continued to rise the authorities were forced to use old ships as temporary prisons and it was in one of these that John Hudson was to spend the next three years of his life. On the River Thames over six hundred convicts were confined in this way – working ashore each day in chains and returning to the hulks each night.

As time passed conditions aboard the hulks became unbearable. Convicts were given very little food, their drinking water – drawn from the river – was impure, and diseases began to spread out of control. In a little over two years more than 170 prisoners died.

Faced with this worsening situation the government decided, in 1786, to renew the system of transportation and elected to ship the convicts to Botany Bay. Sir Joseph Banks, the famous botanist who had travelled with James Cook on the *Endeavour* some years before, had spoken in glowing terms of this distant land and recommended the establishment of a British colony there.

John Hudson knew nothing of Botany Bay but as he was transferred from the prison ship to the transport *Friendship* early in 1787 he felt a certain optimism. Nothing, he was sure, could be as bad as the life he was leaving behind.

Portsmouth Harbour, where a total of eleven vessels were gathered together, was a scene of enormous activity. Convicts, huddled together in chains and under heavy guard, were brought from hulks and prisons all over England. Everywhere sailors, marines and civilians bustled about loading stores, checking equipment and making ready for the journey ahead.

Chosen to command this First Fleet was a retired naval officer Arthur Phillip, the son of a German teacher of languages and an English woman. Phillip had had previous experience in transporting convicts from Lisbon to Brazil when he served in the Portuguese navy and was regarded as a capable organiser and a good leader. He was appointed Governor of New South Wales and given the task of establishing a colony at Botany Bay.

In his charge were over 750 prisoners – men and women of all ages, and some very young children. Their crimes ranged from petty theft to highway robbery and murder.

After many delays the First Fleet slipped quietly out of Portsmouth at 5 o'clock on the morning of May 13th 1787 and began the long voyage to their new land. In addition to the convicts there were over 550 sailors, marines, officials, wives and children aboard the ships.

The fleet comprised six transports, three stores ships and two naval vessels – the *Sirius*, under the command of Governor Phillip, and the *Supply*.

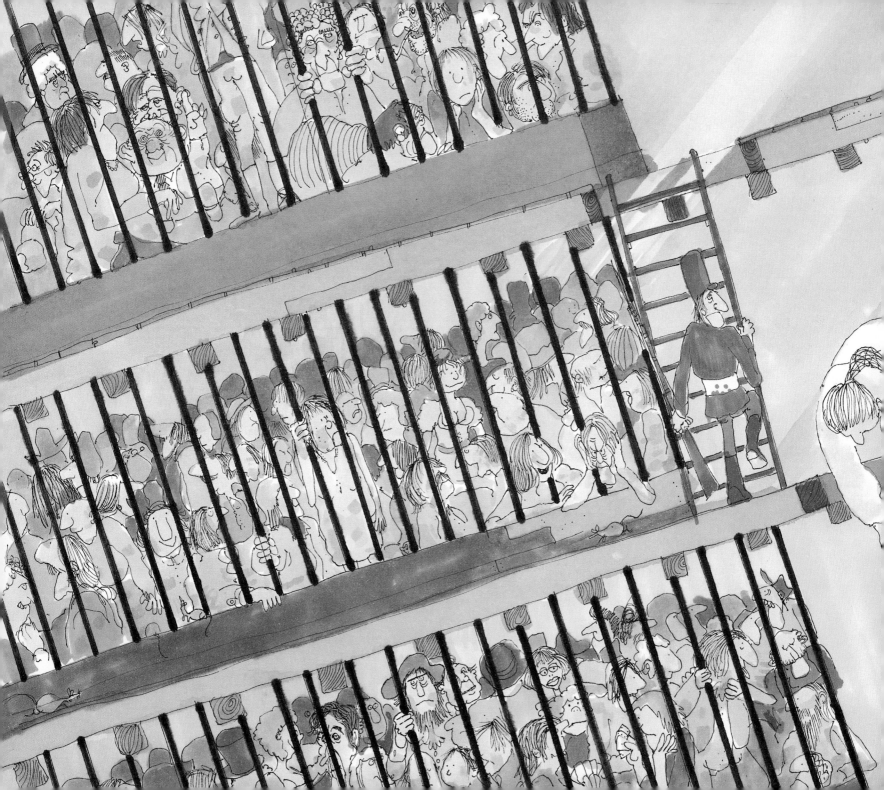

Like many of the convicts John Hudson had
never been to sea before and was not sure what
to expect. At first it was all a great adventure – the
sounds and smells of the ship were new and
exciting but gradually excitement turned to
boredom as one day followed another.

Below decks conditions were little better than
on the hulks. Confined as they were in cramped
spaces where the air was stale and where rats,
cockroaches and bugs abounded the prisoners
frequently fought amongst themselves. The worst
offenders were flogged and placed in irons on the
open decks.

They reached their first port of call, Tenerife in the Canary Islands, on June 3rd. For most of the prisoners it was their first glimpse of a foreign port.

The fleet remained at anchor in Santa Cruz harbour for a week taking on supplies of fresh meat, fruit and vegetables. By this time it was extremely hot and water rationing was introduced. In the ships, attempts were made to sweeten the air by the use of gunpowder explosions but all efforts to improve the ventilation failed and prisoners were continually fainting in the oppressive heat.

From Tenerife the fleet sailed for Rio de Janeiro and, catching favourable trade winds, reached that port in early August.

Here provisions were found to be moderately-priced and plentiful. Exotic fruits such as guavas, pineapples, coconuts and bananas, which many of the First Fleeters had never seen before, were readily available. To their delight the prisoners were allowed the run of the decks, under supervision, whilst the officers went ashore. They remained almost a month in Rio repairing sails, renewing food supplies, airing camping equipment and collecting a variety of plants and seeds they hoped to grow in the new colony.

Leaving Rio the fleet encountered some of the worst weather of the voyage as they crossed the South Atlantic ocean. Gale force winds whipped the seas into a frenzy and convicts and crew alike suffered terribly from sea-sickness. Huge waves crashed constantly over the decks drenching everyone aboard. With only one blanket each Hudson and his fellow convicts were continually racked with cold.

There were many occasions when even the most hardened sailors feared for their lives for anyone washed overboard would have no chance of surviving.

For those unused to the ways of the seas the noise and violent motion were terrifying in the extreme.

On October 13th they arrived at Table Bay at the Cape of Good Hope where they made good the damage caused by the heavy seas and took on additional livestock including horses, cattle, sheep, goats and chickens.

Leaving Table Bay in November the fleet set out on the last and longest leg of the journey. Anxious to make good time Governor Phillip transferred from *Sirius* to the faster ship *Supply* and with the transports *Alexander*, *Scarborough* and *Friendship* sailed ahead of the fleet.

In the middle of the Indian Ocean they spent their first Christmas Day away from England.

Seven weeks after leaving the Cape of Good Hope the advance party rounded Van Diemen's Land and on January 18th arrived at Botany Bay, a mere two days ahead of the rest of the fleet.

The land here appeared grim and inhospitable so, sailing even further north, Phillip discovered Port Jackson where the entire fleet anchored on January 26th, 1788. A landing party was sent ashore, and the British flag unfurled whilst the marines fired volleys into the air. Toasts were drunk to the health of the new colony.

Work began immediately on clearing the ground and within days tents were set up to house the officers, marines and convicts. Governor Phillip named the settlement Sydney in honour of the British Home Secretary.

The voyage had taken over eight months and covered about 24,000 kilometres. More than forty people had died since the fleet left England and seven babies had been born.

When he stepped ashore in New South Wales John Hudson was 13 years old.

As they settled down in their new surroundings Phillip and his men began to realise the enormity of the task ahead. Many of the convicts were too old to work whilst others were too sick or too lazy. The tools they brought from England proved inadequate for the harsh conditions, their plants and seeds failed to grow and wild dingoes made off with many of their sheep and poultry.

For over two years they struggled to survive on the remains of the stores they'd brought with them.

On June 3rd, 1790, with the new colony close to starvation and with many of the original convicts dead or seriously ill, the first ship of the second fleet, the *Lady Juliana*, sailed into Port Jackson with relief supplies and more convicts.

In 1791 John Hudson was given his freedom. He later received a grant of land and settled down to become a respected member of the community.

etween the years of 1791 and 1813 the new colony grew rapidly. Not only did the number of people increase, but farming, and especially grazing, began to occupy much of the available land.

The settlement could not expand to the west because of the great, seemingly impassable mountain range. The mountains were surrounded by a blue haze, from which they took their name.

No-one knew what lay on the other side of the mountains. Until Matthew Flinders sailed around Australia many believed the land was divided by a sea. Flinders established that it was in fact one vast continent, which led settlers to imagine what could be in the centre — a desert, an enormous lake or an inland sea? Some convicts believed China or Paradise to be on the other side of the Blue Mountains.

Many attempts were made to cross the mountains, but until 1813 all had failed.

THE CROSSING OF THE
BLUE MOUNTAINS

n May 1813 a party of men set out from Sydney on a journey which was to alter the course of Australian history. Their success in finding a path across the Blue Mountains opened the way for the country to become more than just a prison colony.

After the arrival of the First Fleet in 1788, conditions in newly settled Sydney Cove were extremely difficult. As later fleets brought more convicts and settlers, food became scarce and a weary Governor Phillip was almost convinced that the colony could not survive on food produced by convict labour alone. Free farm land was offered to people willing to travel to Sydney. Grants of land were also made to military officers and to convicts who had completed their sentences.

any early attempts at farming were unsuccessful. Seeds, trees and plants brought from England and other places often failed to survive in the harsh conditions and most of the tools proved to be inadequate.

Gradually, however, crops began to grow, food became more plentiful and farmers were able to trade their produce at public stores for other essential goods. Convicts were allowed to work on farms and were paid in rations of food and rum. In time, many officers and some ex-convicts became wealthy and respected.

In 1791 John Macarthur arrived in Sydney as a member of the New South Wales Corps. Macarthur was a man of ideas and before long he was experimenting with ways to improve farming methods. Soon he was successfully growing vegetables, grain crops, fruit and vines, in addition to raising pigs, cattle and poultry. His main contribution, however, was the introduction into the country of merino sheep, which he grazed on his property near Sydney.

These sheep produced wool of the finest quality which Macarthur sold to the spinning mills in England to be made into clothes. Many of these clothes were later shipped to the new colony to be sold to settlers or issued to convicts, some of whom may have worked on the very farms where the wool had been produced.

Crops were becoming risky as seasons were often spoiled by droughts, floods or plagues of insects. Gradually more and more settlers turned to sheep farming as a way of making a living. As there was a steady demand for wool in England the big landowners wanted even more land for their growing flocks and other farmers were also insisting on their share for agriculture.

arlier, several attempts had been made to cross the Blue Mountains – Francis Barrallier reported finding a way across in 1802 but no notice was taken of his report. Botanist George Cayley tried several times without success and declared that the expansion of the colony beyond the mountains was impossible. Others, however, including Gregory Blaxland, a wealthy farmer from England, remained convinced that the much-needed new pasture lay just beyond the mountain range.

Blaxland lost many cattle as a result of the drought and was determined to find new grazing land rather than see the rest of his stock die of starvation. Governor Lachlan Macquarie was anxious to keep the settlement confined because he feared the convicts would escape. He eventually gave reluctant permission for Blaxland and two other landowners, William Charles Wentworth and William Lawson, to mount an expedition.

To make their task a little easier they each took along a convict servant. An experienced bushman was added to the party and, on 11 May 1813 they set off from Blaxland's farm with their pack horses laden with provisions and accompanied by five hunting dogs.

Earlier explorers had tried to find a way through the mountains by using the many valleys and gorges, but Blaxland's party planned to follow a route along the ridges. The going was hard and progress slow. For mile after mile they hacked their way through thick, almost impenetrable brush, often running into dead ends, having to backtrack and start all over again. On bad days they covered less than two miles before collapsing exhausted for a few hours uneasy sleep. After more than a week of this backbreaking, frustrating work they came across a mound of stones possibly left some years earlier by George Bass.

For nearly three weeks they pushed westwards, slashing a path for the horses; sometimes having to unload the provisions when the ground became too steep for the animals to stay on their feet. In parts, the scrub was so thick the explorers were barely able to see more than three or four feet ahead. The branches tore at their clothes and ripped their skin and, at all times, they were in constant fear of attack by unfriendly Aborigines. This fear, however, was unfounded and the only other living things they saw were bandicoots and, occasionally, a kangaroo, crow or cockatoo.

On 31 May, their food almost gone, their shoes and clothes practically in shreds and themselves near the point of collapse, the party ascended Mt. York, crossed Cox's River and, climbing a sugarloaf shaped hill, later to be named Mt. Blaxland, they saw what they'd so often dreamed about. In Blaxland's own words "all around, forest and grass land, sufficient in extent to support the stock of the Colony for the next thirty years".

Blowed
if I know...

Exhausted, but elated at their find, the men set about the return journey to Sydney. They had not actually completed the crossing but with their supplies almost finished they had little choice but to turn back. In any event the way was now open for others to follow and at least they knew what lay beyond the mountain chain. The return journey took only six days and they arrived back in South Creek with no food apart from a little flour.

ack in Sydney the news of their success spread quickly and they were greeted with great jubilation. A newspaper of the day proclaimed:

"THE BLUE MOUNTAINS CONQUERED: A NOTABLE FEAT".
Governor Macquarie offered each of the three explorers a grant
of 1,000 acres of land of their own choosing.

Following the success of Blaxland's party, Governor Macquarie ordered a further expedition in November 1813. Led by George Evans, a government surveyor, this group was able to follow the path of Blaxland, pushing on a further 100 miles and in doing so crossing the Great Dividing Range. Evans discovered and named the Fish and Macquarie Rivers and at the same time came across a huge grass-covered plain near the present site of Bathurst. When Evans returned to Sydney with glowing reports of this fertile land he'd found, the Governor ordered that a road be built.

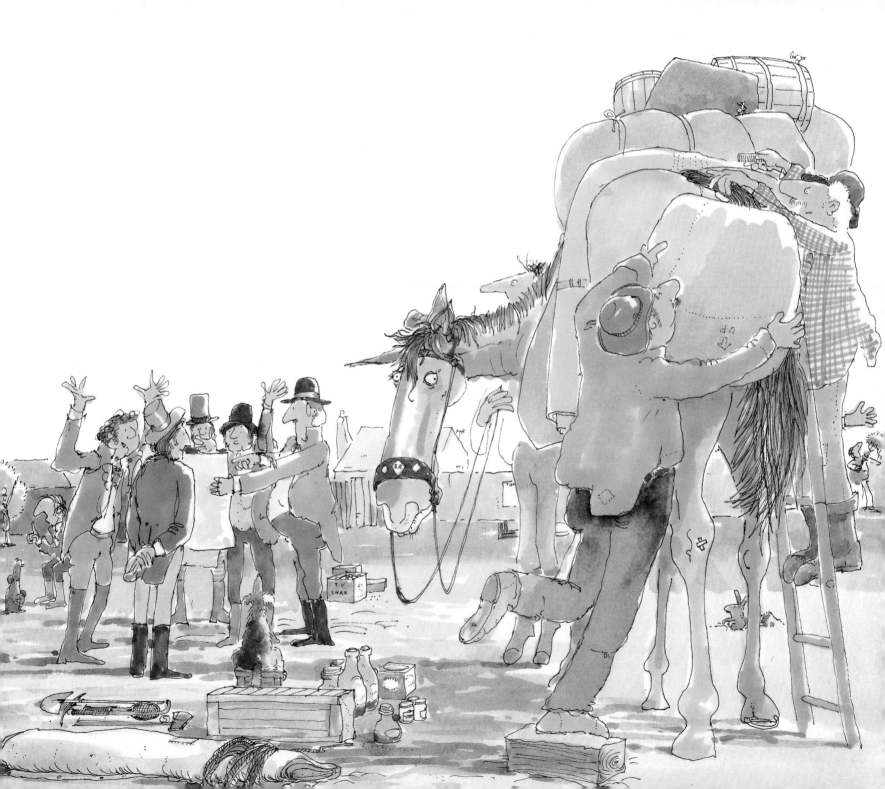

A former army officer, William Cox, was chosen for this task and, with a work gang of only thirty convicts, he turned Evans' primitive path into a usable road in less than six months. Macquarie was delighted with the results and, with much pomp and ceremony, led a procession along the new road in April 1815 and formally proclaimed the founding of the town of Bathurst.

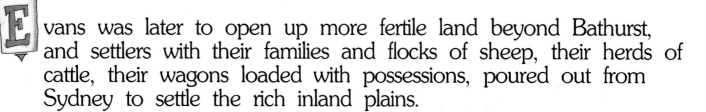

Evans was later to open up more fertile land beyond Bathurst, and settlers with their families and flocks of sheep, their herds of cattle, their wagons loaded with possessions, poured out from Sydney to settle the rich inland plains.

he way to the west had been unlocked and a great new era in Australian history had begun.

Crossing the Blue Mountains was one of the first of many steps that led to the expansion of the colony. Following in the footsteps of Blaxland, Wentworth and Lawson were other successful explorers who opened up the country.

Many free settlers arrived in Australia, to settle or squat on land and take up farming activities. Wool and wheat became important sources of income for the colony.

Gradually, Britain abandoned convict transportation. By 1852 no convicts were sent to New South Wales, Victoria or Tasmania. And in 1868 the system was finally abolished in Western Australia.

In 1849 Edward Hargraves returned to Sydney from the Californian goldfields, convinced that there was gold in Australia. In 1851 he crossed the Blue Mountains and found gold.

Soon after, gold was discovered near Ballarat, and the rush was on. But not without problems.

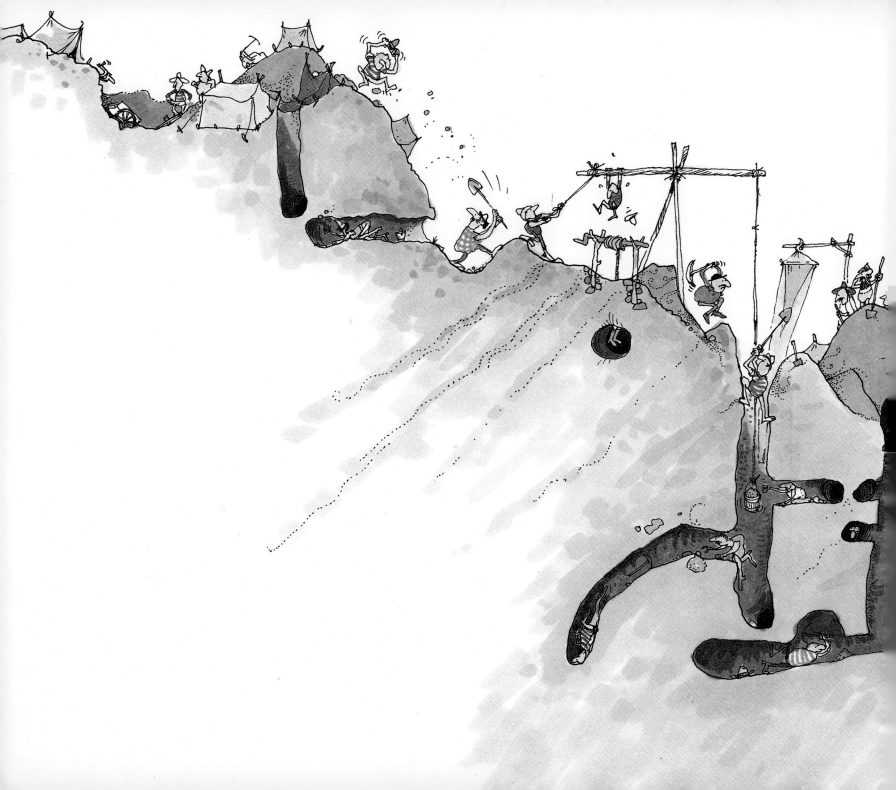

EUREKA STOCKADE

In 1848 gold was discovered in America. In that year, and the one that followed, prospectors from all over the world flocked to California to seek their fortunes in the "Great Gold Rush".

Two years later in sleepy Buninyong near Ballarat, Victoria, another gold rush began.

Until then, the main visitors to Ballarat had been sheep but with the discovery of gold in 1851 people came from everywhere in the hope of finding quick riches.

They came from England, Ireland, Germany, Italy, America and China, as well as all parts of Australia.

Sailors deserted their ships, shopkeepers left their stores and servants ran away from their masters.

They set up their tents and began digging in the hard ground in search of gold. Everyone was equal — gentlemen, labourers, farmers, ex-convicts and sons of noblemen.

The work was hard and many miners gave up after a couple of months and returned home still poor.

Others were luckier and found huge nuggets worth more money than they'd ever imagined.

By law, Queen Victoria owned all of the land in Australia and the Governor decided that for the privilege of mining and keeping the gold they found, the miners should pay a licence fee of thirty shillings a month.

This licence fee had to be paid by all miners whether they found gold or not and the miners thought it was unfair — especially the unlucky ones.

The Gold Commissioner sent troopers after the miners to make sure they all had licences. This caused a good deal of ill-feeling and often fights broke out between troopers and miners.

In October 1854 a miner named Scobie was murdered near the Eureka Hotel. The diggers felt that the hotel-keeper, Bentley, was guilty of the murder and when the charges against him were dropped they burned down the hotel.

Later at a public meeting on Bakery Hill the miners formed the Ballarat Reform League and sent a deputation to the Governor demanding the right to vote, better conditions and the abolition of licence fees. The Governor refused their demands.

Instead he sent soldiers and mounted police to Ballarat to enforce the law.

The miners responded by building a stockade to separate themselves from the police and troopers. They armed themselves against a possible attack, elected Peter Lalor as their leader and burned their licences.

Inside the stockade the miners raised their new flag, featuring the Southern Cross on a blue background.
 The flag became known as the Eureka Flag.

The soldiers called on the miners to leave the stockade but they refused to do so.

At dawn on Sunday December 3, the troops attacked the stockade and, in the firing that followed, at least 30 miners were killed and 128 taken prisoner. Four soldiers died in the attack.

With the exception of Peter Lalor, who escaped during the fighting,
the leaders of the miners were later tried for treason but the charges

were dismissed by the court and the men allowed to go free.

Following this the monthly licences were dropped and for a fee of £1 a year the miners were given the right to vote and mine for gold.

In 1855 Peter Lalor was elected to the Victorian Parliament, where he represented the interests of the people of Ballarat and brought about many improvements in their conditions.

The men who died at Eureka retain a unique place in Australian history. A monument to their memory now stands at Ballarat.